SPIDERS

First published in Canada by Whitecap Books
351 Lynn Avenue, North Vancouver, British Columbia, V7J 2C4

ISBN 1-55285-127-3

Children's Publisher: Linsay Knight
Series Editor: Marie-Louise Taylor
Managing Editor: Loretta Barnard
Art Director: Carolyn Hewitson
Design concept: Stan Lamond
Production Manager: Linda Watchorn

Illustrator: Frank Knight
Consultant: Dr Robert Raven
Writer: Dr Robert Raven
Educational Consultant: Pamela Hook

Film separation by Pica Colour Separation Overseas Pte Ltd, Singapore
Printed in Hong Kong by Sing Cheong Printing Co. Ltd.

When you see a word in **bold** type, you'll find its meaning in the Glossary at the back of the book.

INVESTIGATE

SPIDERS

Consultant **Dr Robert Raven**
Illustrator **Frank Knight**

CONTENTS

CONTENTS

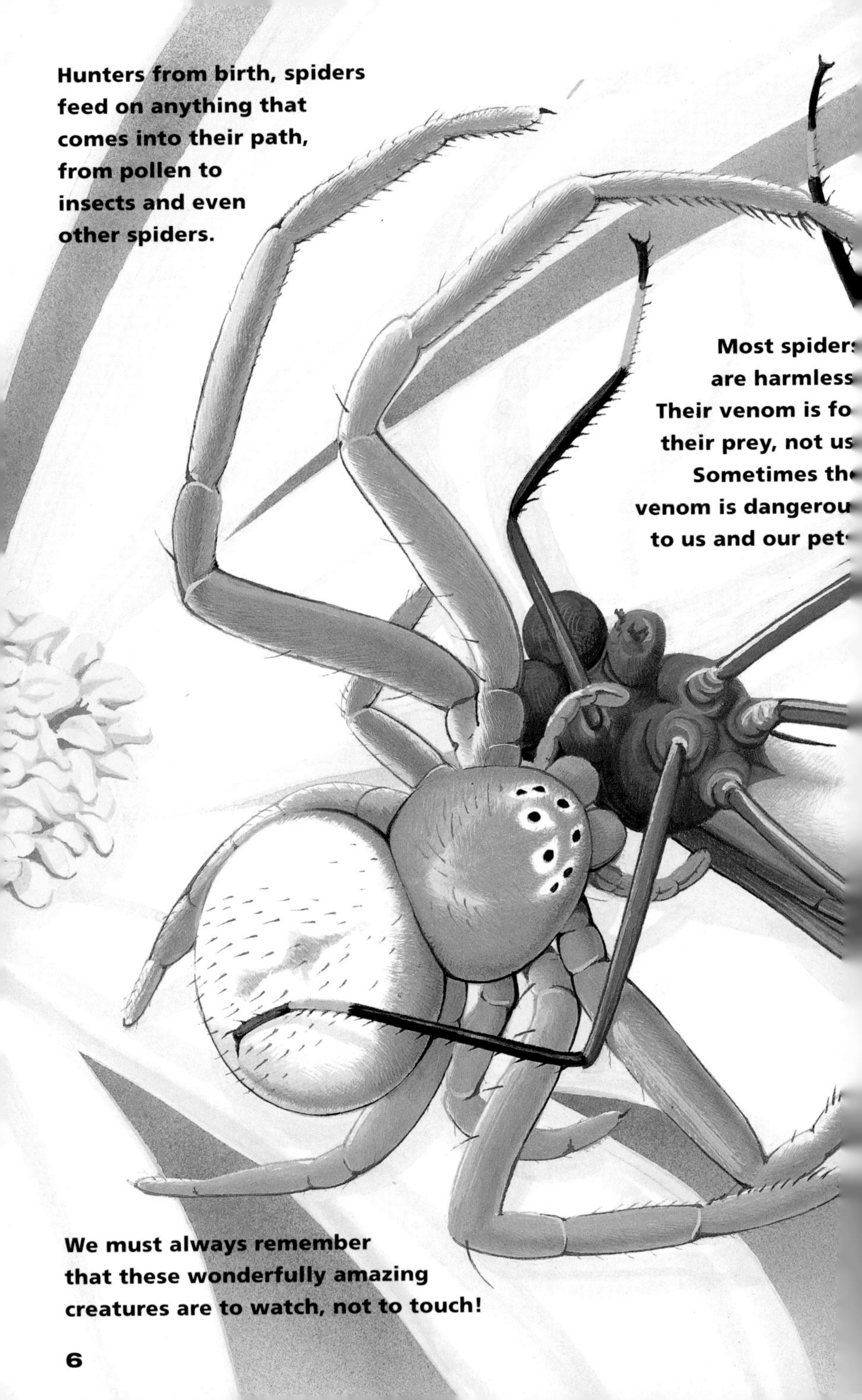

Hunters from birth, spiders feed on anything that comes into their path, from pollen to insects and even other spiders.

Most spider
are harmless
Their venom is fo
their prey, not us
Sometimes th
venom is dangerou
to us and our pet

We must always remember that these wonderfully amazing creatures are to watch, not to touch!

Friend, foe or fable?

On a balmy autumn morning, the air fills with fine lines of silk. Some float and others fall to the ground or cover the bushes. At the end of each line is a tiny ***spiderling,*** *one of millions about to set off on a journey away from its mother.*

A SPIDER'S WORLD

Spiders have explored many different ways of living—from hiding in tubes in the ground to building beautiful and complicated webs or pouncing on their prey from afar. They have adapted marvellous ways to use the gifts they have—silk, venom and even behaviour. Some hide by sticking soil on their bodies. Some look like other animals, such as wasps and ants. From inside to outside, spiders have body parts that are specially useful for the particular life they lead. Some have big eyes, some have long legs, some have padded feet. They use all these things to help keep insects from getting out of control.

LOOK AGAIN!

The spider is hard to see because it is the same colour as the petals of the flower.

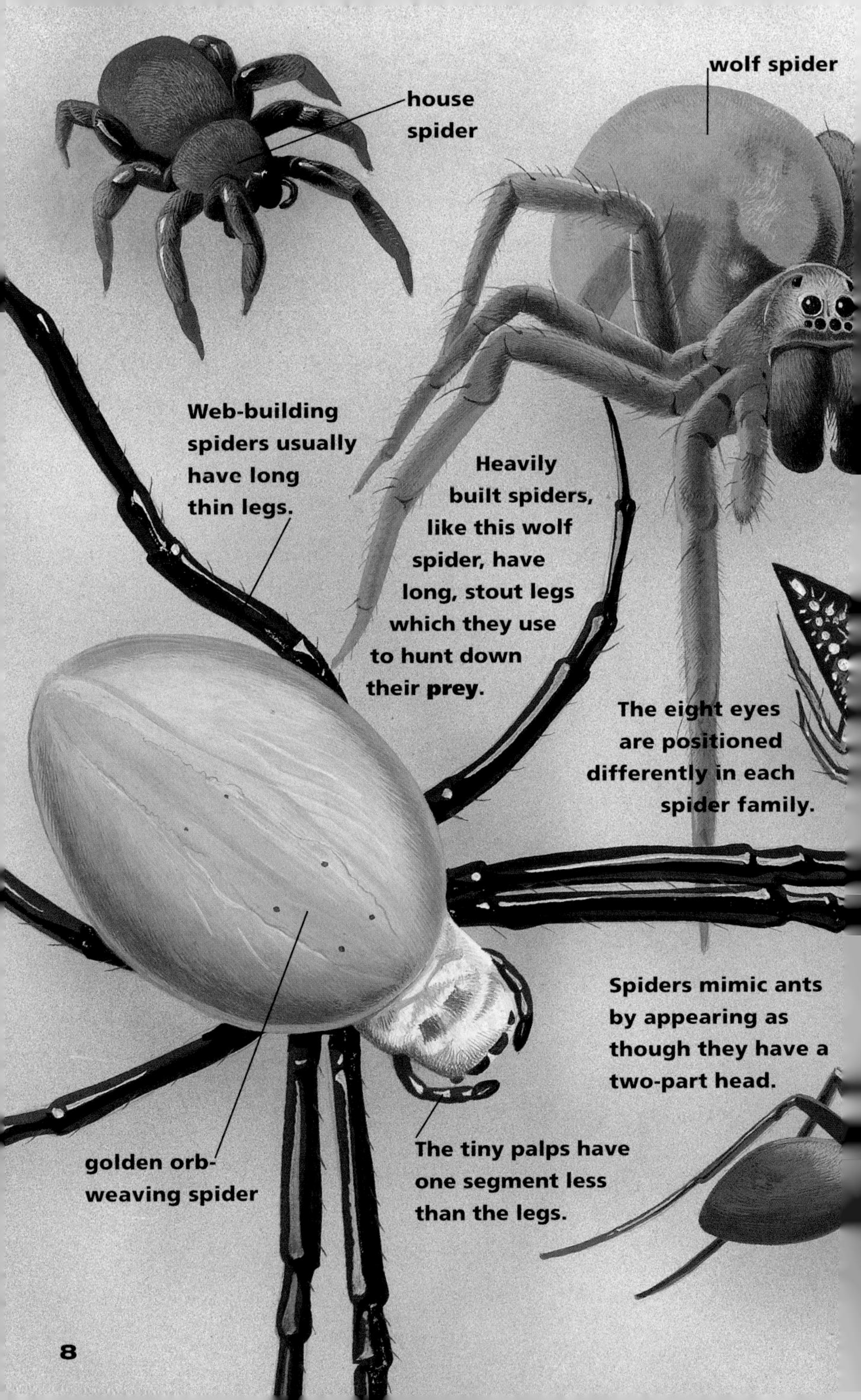
house spider
wolf spider
Web-building spiders usually have long thin legs.
Heavily built spiders, like this wolf spider, have long, stout legs which they use to hunt down their **prey**.
The eight eyes are positioned differently in each spider family.
Spiders mimic ants by appearing as though they have a two-part head.
golden orb-weaving spider
The tiny palps have one segment less than the legs.

What is a spider?

Spiders are eight-legged animals with a two-part body, silk-making organs, and venom-injecting prongs called fangs. They belong to a group called the Arachnida (arachnids). They are found deep in the ground, under the sea, on land and in the air. Some are found as high as the jets fly!

SPIDER, INSECT OR CRAB?

Spiders' legs are attached to the head (**cephalothorax**), as are a pair of short, leg-like limbs called **palps**. So are the **chelicerae**, which are like jaws. The body or abdomen is just a soft bag. Insects have a three-part body, only six legs and a pair of antennae. Crabs have a shell-like body, all in one part.

triangular spider

Some spiders look like ants or even smell like them. Ants are so common that it is a great advantage to mimic them. Such spiders eat ants while they hunt with them!

SRI-LANKAN WEAVER ANT

nt-like umping spider

Evolution

Spiders are among the first animals to live on Earth. Even long ago, there were many different spiders with many ways of feeding, and over time, they developed strong silk webs and more powerful venom.

OLDER THAN DINOSAURS

Spiders were around before the dinosaurs—they evolved 300 million years ago, and most families we see today were around over 100 million years ago. Even then there were web spinners. Spiders quick developed many clever hunting methods. Spiders that were trapped in amber in the Baltic and Dominican Republic 40 to 60 million years ago look just like those alive today. Spiders experimented with every structure, but four changes were the most important. Large eyes gave long range sight. Pads of hairs beside the claws ensured that spiders could walk on all surfaces. The silk was always a safety line and the venom stopped prey from struggling too long.

The world's biggest spider was a trapdoor called *Megarachne servinei,* from the Upper Carboniferous period (320 million years ago). It lived in Argentina and had a leg span of about 50 centimetres (20 inches)!

SPIDER FOSSIL

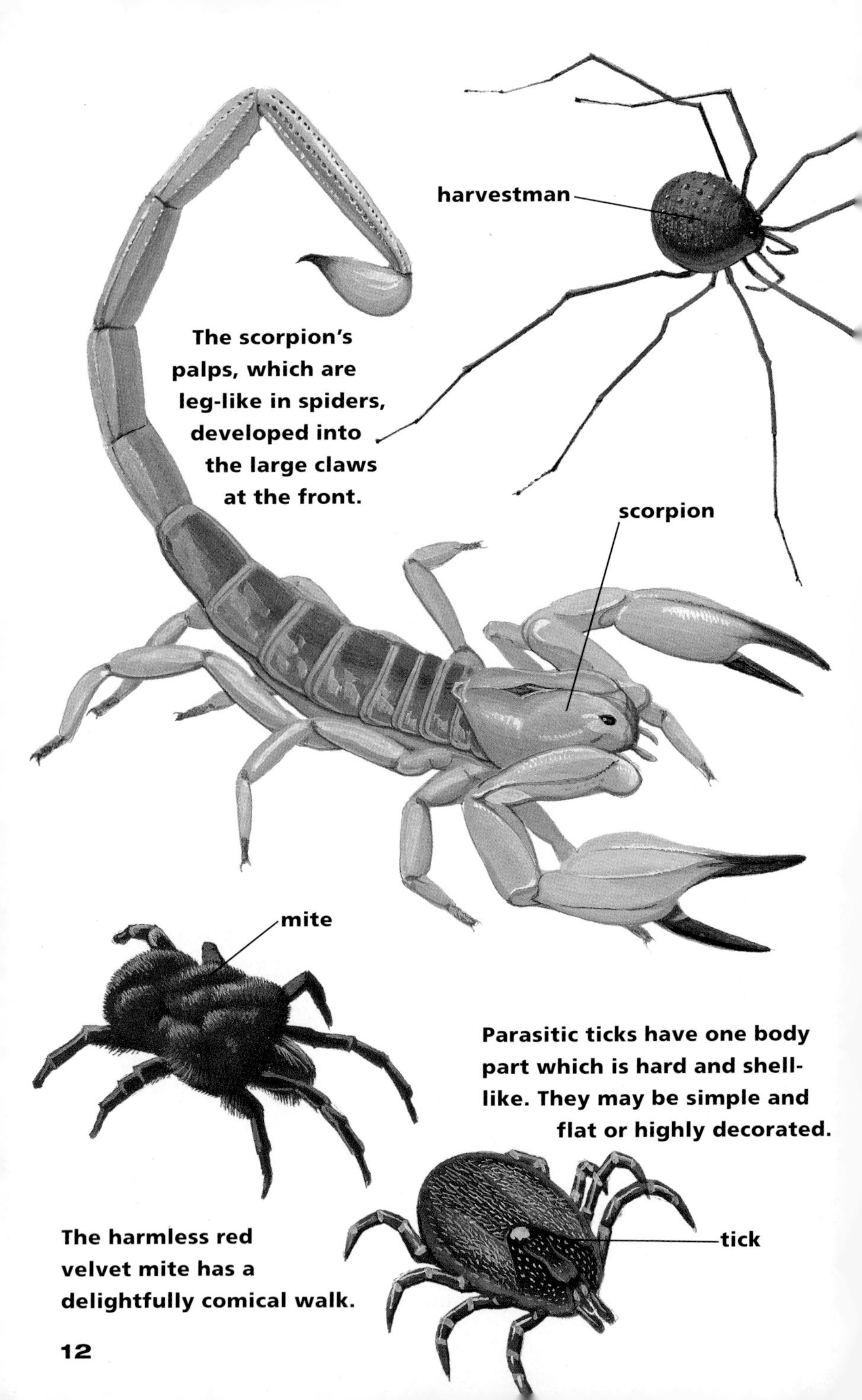

The scorpion's palps, which are leg-like in spiders, developed into the large claws at the front.

Parasitic ticks have one body part which is hard and shell-like. They may be simple and flat or highly decorated.

The harmless red velvet mite has a delightfully comical walk.

Even spiders have relatives

Other arachnids include scorpions, ticks, mites, harvestmen and strange marine matchstick animals. Fossils show us that scorpion-like creatures walked the sea floors. King crabs and matchstick animals still live in the sea.

SPIDER COUSINS

Mites explore deserts, seas, lakes and streams. In deserts, long worm-like mites slither through the tiny spaces between sand grains. Some mites live in the minute cavities inside leaves. Mites have only a single body part, unlike spiders which have two. Scorpions are larger than most spiders. They have a long tail with a venomous sting at the tip and large pincers, which they use to hold and tear at their prey.

Harvestmen have one part to the body, no tail and tiny chelicerae. They are also called daddy long-legs.

Most spider relatives do not inject venom with their fangs. The biting chelicerae in most are reduced to small crab-like claws. Over millions of years, ticks and mites changed their behaviour. They became parasites, hanging on to another animal and feeding from it. The chelicerae developed into a pair of long barbed spears to pierce and hold onto the prey and to inject venom.

TICK

ENGORGED TICK

The outside of a spider

Spiders have two body parts. The hard outer skeleton (cuticle) of the spider's legs and head are attached to the soft bag-like abdomen by a narrow waist. The cuticle is strong and flexible because, like plywood, it has many layers.

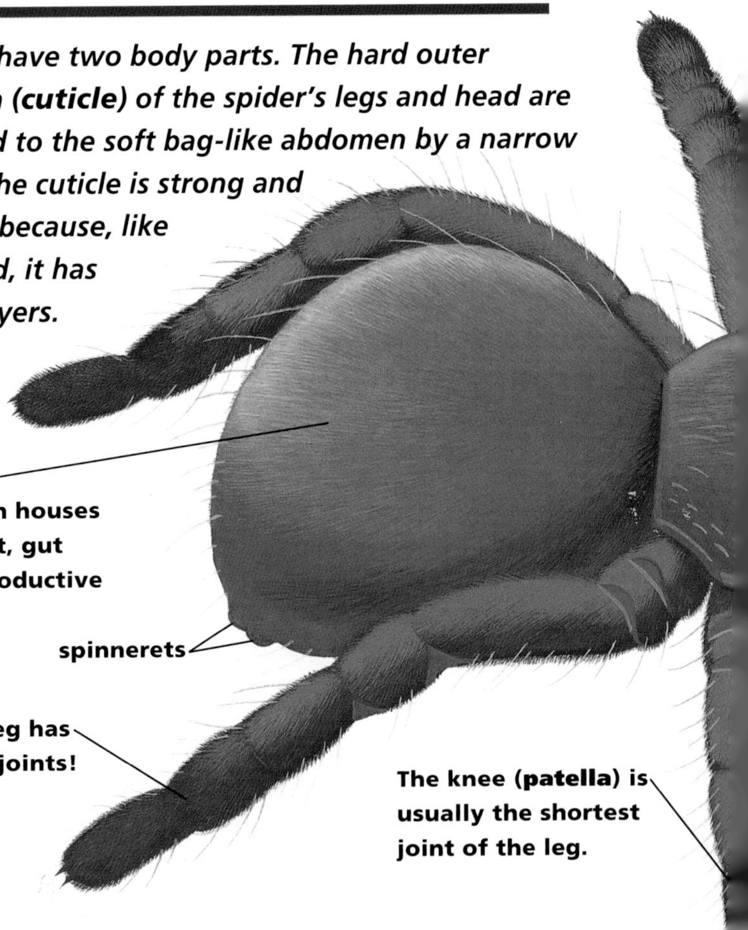

The soft abdomen houses the heart, gut and reproductive organs.

spinnerets

Each leg has seven joints!

The knee (patella) is usually the shortest joint of the leg.

SENSATIONAL SPINNERETS

At the end of the abdomen are usually three pairs of openings, called **spinnerets**, through which silk is pulled out. Sometimes there are four pairs and sometimes only one. Each kind of spinneret makes one or more different types of silk. One kind makes egg sacs (males don't have those), one wraps food, another makes the web or stops the spider from falling too far or too fast.

Legs have different hairs in different places. The hairs on top are sensitive to wind. The fat hairs underneath are for holding slippery food.

Claw tufts hold prey when the spider is feeding. They also allow the spider to climb vertically and upside down, even on smooth surfaces like glass.

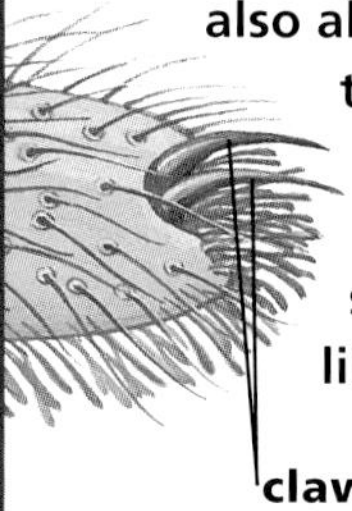

claw tufts

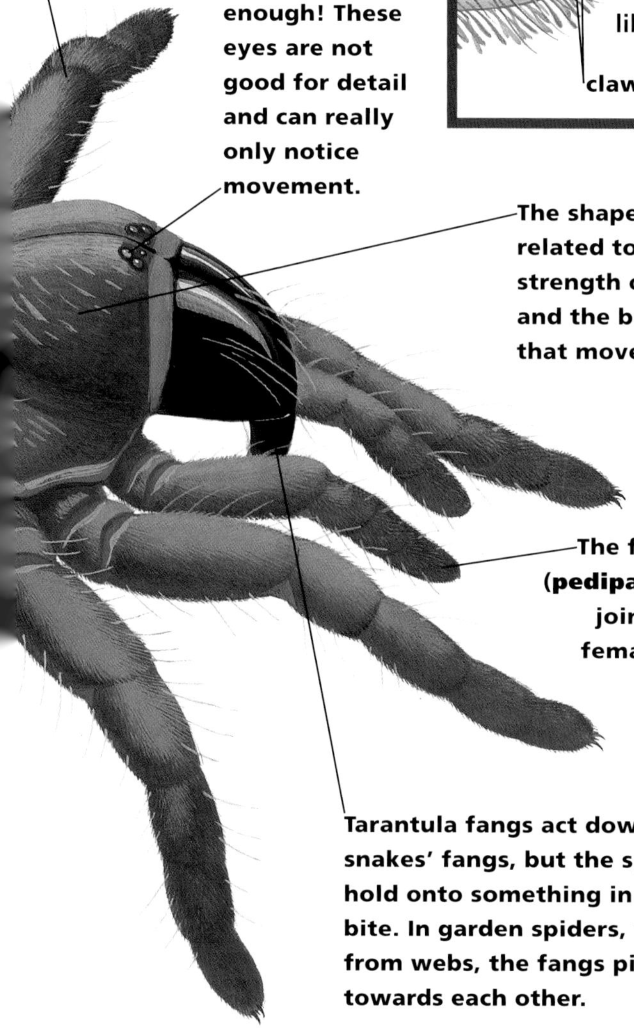

Eight eyes on spiders are not enough! These eyes are not good for detail and can really only notice movement.

The shape of the head is related to the size and strength of the fangs and the big chelicerae that move them.

The front shorter limbs (pedipalps) have one less joint than the legs. In females, they look like short legs.

Tarantula fangs act downwards like snakes' fangs, but the spider must hold onto something in order to bite. In garden spiders, which hang from webs, the fangs pinch towards each other.

The inside of a spider

The head (cephalothorax) contains the 'brain', stomach, venom, some tiny waste outlets and lots of muscles attached to an inner plate. The abdomen contains the heart, lungs, intestines and the silk glands.

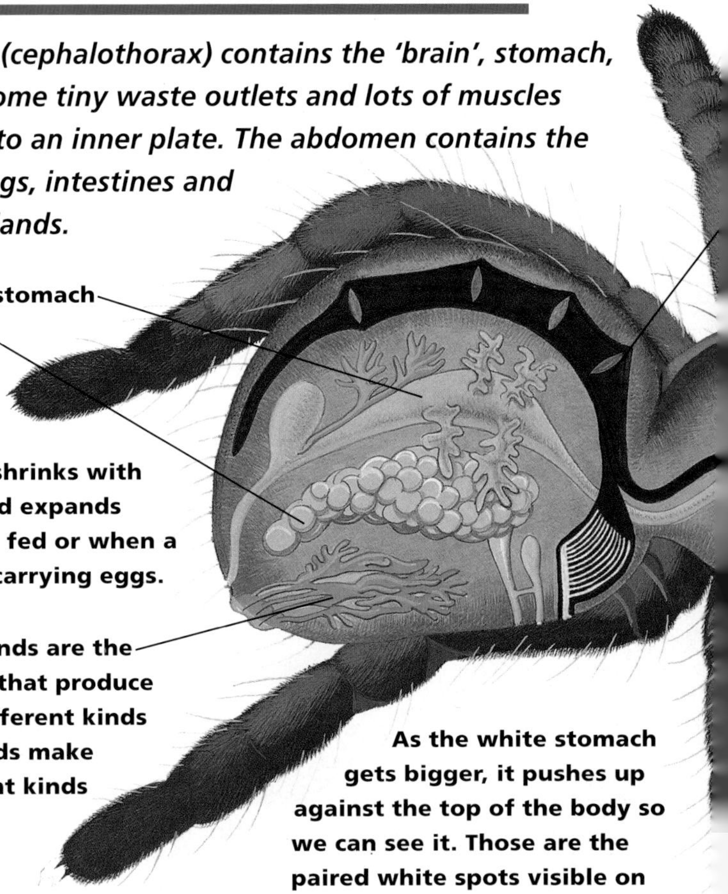

stomach

eggs

The body shrinks with hunger and expands when well fed or when a female is carrying eggs.

Silk glands are the organs that produce silk. Different kinds of glands make different kinds of silk.

As the white stomach gets bigger, it pushes up against the top of the body so we can see it. Those are the paired white spots visible on the body of many spiders.

BLOOD AND GUTS

Blood passes from the heart to the lungs and then into the rest of the body. It carries oxygen to the muscles and other parts of the body. One-fifth of the body weight is blood! Tarantulas have two sets of lungs—the front lungs provide oxygen to the head; the back lungs provide oxygen to the rest of the body. In other spiders, air feeds into the abdomen by fine tubes opening near the spinnerets.

The heart beats fast in hunting spiders. They can only run for a short distance because the tiny waist cannot supply enough blood for prolonged movement.

Book lungs are the two (or four) patches that are underneath the spider's body. They have many thin leaves, like a book, and help the spider to breathe.

book lungs

venom gland

The brain (not shown) is a large mass around the stomach and blood vessels. It is a central nervous system, controlling all the body's functions.

The mouth is tucked away between the palps.

Most spider blood is milky or light blue, but in some huntsmen it is green!

The legs are tubes of muscles surrounded by blood.

h blood ssure ps the ider to tend its legs d claws, to np, to moult to mate.

Even the spines move when the blood pressure in the legs rises!

LOOK AGAIN!

The groove on the spider's head is caused by the sucking stomach muscles!

Bright eyes!

The number, size, shape and position of spiders' eyes varies between families. Cave spiders have no eyes. Hunters have big eyes. Web builders sense with their legs, so their eyes are small. Scientists can often tell what family a spider comes from just by looking at how the eyes are arranged.

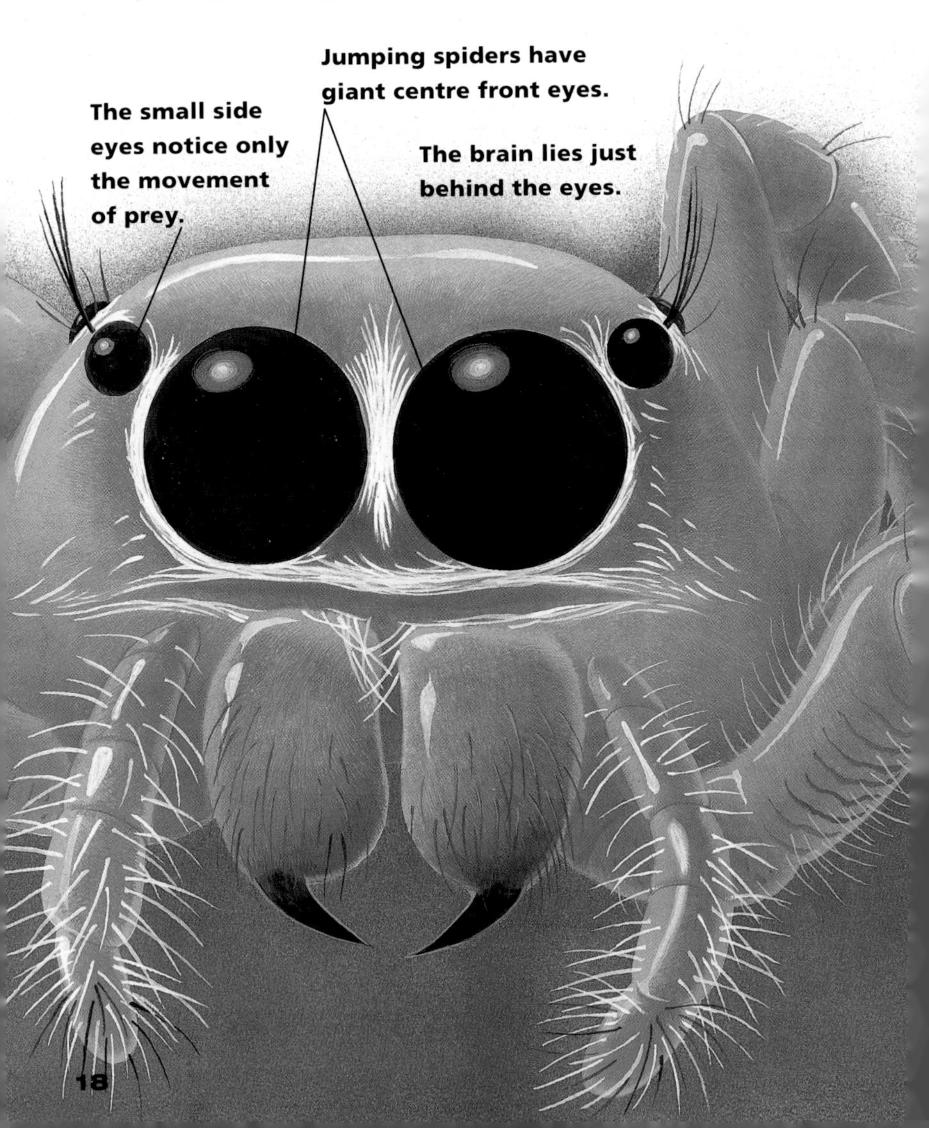

ALL THE BETTER TO SEE YOU WITH

Big eyes allow spiders to see sharply. Usually only two eyes of the eight need to be big. Spiders with large eyes go hunting after their prey. The Australasian jumping spider *(Portia)* has the second best eyesight of any animal known! (An eagle has the best eyesight.) It hunts other spiders on their webs. When jumping spiders meet, they perform fancy dances to signal who they are. If they are males they fight. If they are male and female of the same species, they watch each other do a mating dance. Jumping spiders can turn their head to look at you.

Together, the two main eyes of a jumping spider are bigger than its brain!

The garden spider has small eyes. It relies on other senses to catch its food.

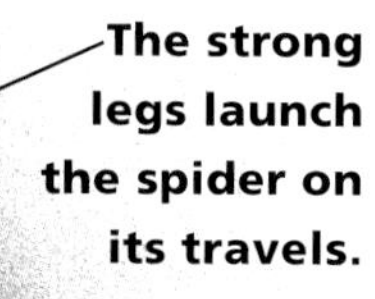

Most spiders' eyes are small and notice only movement, light and darkness. The tugging of an insect in the web tells the spider where its food is.

Female funnelwebs have strong legs that push and pull them down steep burrows.

The body of the female is fat with eggs.

LOOK AGAIN!

If you blow on spiders they get upset. Why? (The answer is elsewhere in this book.)

Female spiders have leg-like palps and their short strong legs all look the same.

female funnel-web

The male hardly feeds at all and its body is small.

Male funnelwebs have longer legs. They walk far in search of females. Funnelwebs, trapdoors and tarantulas are mygale spiders. Mygales are large spiders with big, straight jaws.

male funnel-web

The fourth leg of widow spiders has a 'comb' for throwing silk at prey.

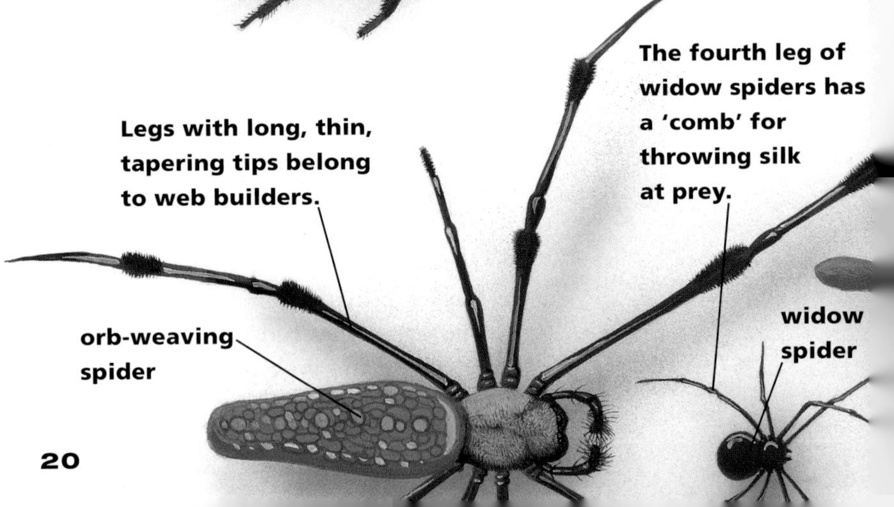

Legs with long, thin, tapering tips belong to web builders.

orb-weaving spider

widow spider

Getting around

Legs are not just a means of moving. Spiders can also fly! The legs are covered with different kinds of highly sensitive hairs. They are more important than eyes. You can tell what family a spider belongs to just by its legs.

LEGS THAT SEE AND SING

Long delicate hairs on the legs tell the spider about wind, vibrations and smells. Their position, type and number tells us the family to which a spider belongs. As each leg moves, the brain stores information about direction and distance. Even blind, a spider lured out of its nest when frightened knows the quickest way back to its home. The brain calculates the answer in a flash! Can you do that? Legs also sing! By using the grooves or hairs like Velcro, whistling spiders can make a hiss or a tune. They push their legs together then pull them apart repeatedly.

The palp of adult male spiders is modified for mating. The claw is bulb-shaped, like a bottle, to hold the sperm. The shape of the bulb is different for every species.

PALP OF MALE TARANTULA

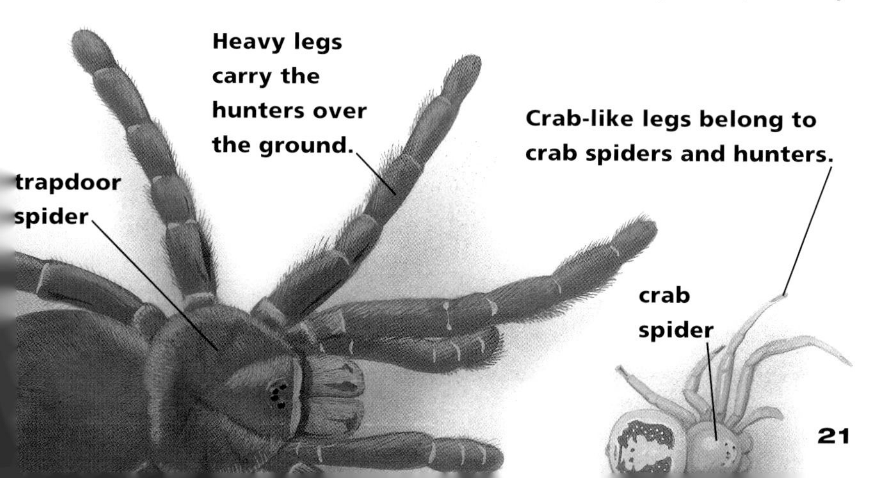

Fangs!

Fangs are like sharp curved needles that the spider bites with. They inject venom into the prey. Time has changed spider venom to make it stronger. Strong venom stops prey from destroying the spider's web or hurting the spider.

SIDEWAYS OR DOWN?

The fangs of some spiders, such as trapdoor spiders, strike down and venom drops hang off the fang tips. The spiders must hold the prey and push against it with the big chelicerae that open and move the fangs in and out. Most spiders have fangs that operate sideways and pinch towards each other. Venom is a complex liquid that is different for every species. When venom is injected, the muscles of the prey start to dissolve immediately.

In tarantulas and trapdoors, the venom gland is in the chelicerae which are large and strong. A tube goes from the gland to a hole in the tip of the fang. In web spinners, the venom gland is in the head and the chelicerae are smaller.

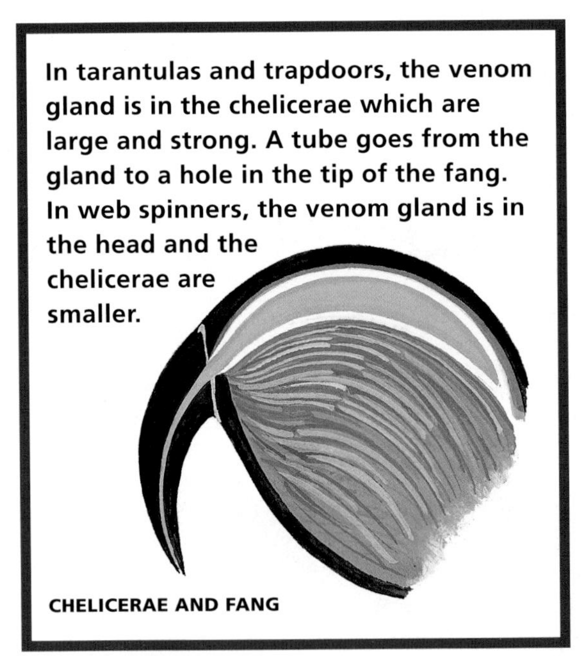

CHELICERAE AND FANG

The fangs pull the prey hard against three rows of teeth under each chelicera. They work almost like scissors. This is as close as spiders get to chewing.

In males, the first and second legs have bumps that help hold the female still and keep her fangs open during mating.

LOOK AGAIN!

When trapdoor spiders mate, the female greets the male in full attack pose!

The red colour shows the location of the covers of the large front book lungs. All trapdoors and tarantulas have a second pair of lungs behind that.

The brush of red hairs under the fangs stops solid bits of food going into the mouth. Spiders can only drink their food. Hard bits would choke them.

One tiny drop of funnelweb venom can kill an adult in fifteen minutes! One teaspoon of venom can kill over 300 monkeys!

The web spider won't touch the red and black beetle. These are nature's warning colours.
LOOK AGAIN!
The crab spider's legs are positioned sideways so it is flat against the flower stalks.

What do spiders eat?

A spider's daily diet includes pollen and nectar, insects, lizards, small birds, mice and bats, other spiders and even their own web. But spiders must be careful—wasps, worms, centipedes, other spiders and even mould are their enemies.

This spider's web is a funnel-shaped tube.

A butterfly has landed on flowers where the crab spider was hiding, and has been caught.

This unsuspecting moth has become the huntsman's dinner!

SOUP AGAIN?

Tiny holes are made by the fangs, and powerful juices flow from the spider into the prey and dissolve insect muscle, gut and brain. The spider's strong stomach sucks out the liquid. So the variety of food might taste different and it must be fun crunching insects, but it is always soup! Of course, a spider can also be food. A flatworm sneaks up, pushes its head into a trapdoor's body and gobbles it up.

Web spiders quickly kill and wrap the food. They can hang it up for a later snack or take it to the centre of the web and eat it fresh!

Hunters

Most spiders sit and wait for food. Others chase it down. Some smell like bad food and attract flies and some fake dying and eat other spiders.

Spiders are like cheetahs. They can run fast only for short distances.

Jumping spiders see long distances, stalking flies from afar.

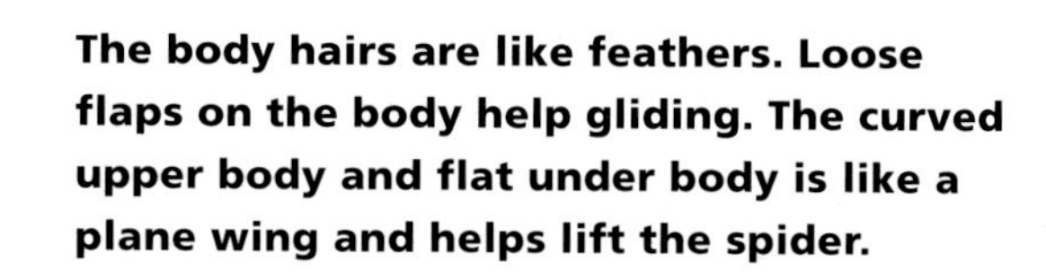

The body hairs are like feathers. Loose flaps on the body help gliding. The curved upper body and flat under body is like a plane wing and helps lift the spider.

A WAITING GAME

Jumping spiders and wolf spiders have good eyesight and go hunting for food. Crab spiders use **camouflage** and hide in the flowers. Others behave as if they are ill—when a giant huntsman approaches thinking to find prey, it becomes prey! Ant-mimics look and some even smell like ants so they can hunt with them and not be noticed. Pirate, white-tailed and pelican spiders just hunt other spiders! Claw tufts, strong spines and strong venom are very important for hunters. Can you think why?

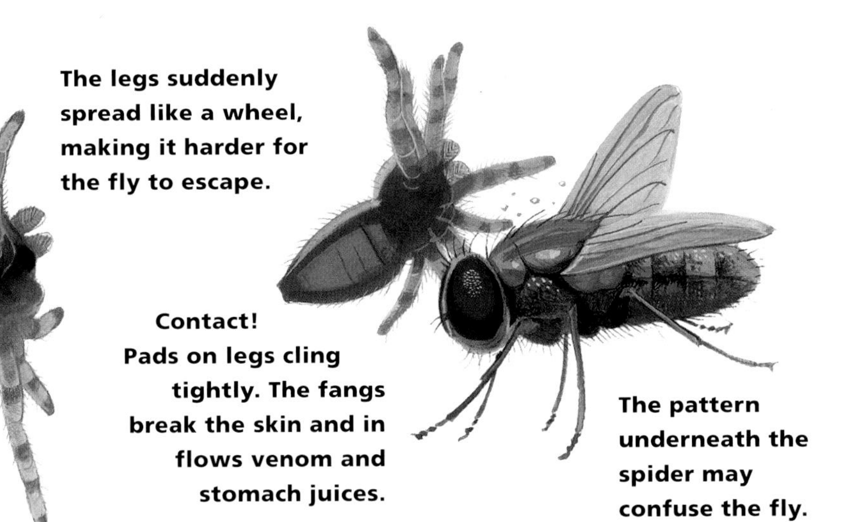

The legs suddenly spread like a wheel, making it harder for the fly to escape.

Contact! Pads on legs cling tightly. The fangs break the skin and in flows venom and stomach juices.

The pattern underneath the spider may confuse the fly.

The sticky silk of the door holds the soil and hides the door.

Trapdoor spiders sit with the legs under the open door and feel the vibrations of the insect walking by.

The hard, sharp body of the jewel spider protects it from predators.

LOOK AGAIN!

If you gently touch a web join with a stick, you will see how strong it is.

The spider uses the springiness of the web to lift up the heavy butterfly. The weight of the butterfly keeps the web stretched. This is important, because a loose web does not catch prey.

Silk spinners

From a single strand of silk to complicated webs, spiders have mastered the wonderful powers of silk—elastic but strong and sticky. There is a different kind of silk for every purpose, and even some for leftovers!

WHAT IS SILK USED FOR?

Silk helps spiders get around. (It is their safety line.) It even carries spiders up where planes fly. Most silk is used for catching and wrapping food, for lining burrows and for protecting eggs. Silk that smells attracts flies, and yellow silk attracts other insects. Many webs have at least three kinds of silk. The first silk laid down is the outer frame of the web and a few spirals. Different silk is used for the inner web and then sticky drops are added to hold prey. Blue silk or band silk is often added for decoration and to attract prey. When the silk is broken the spider pulls in the web, rolls it up and enjoys a satisfying meal of silk, insects and even pollen.

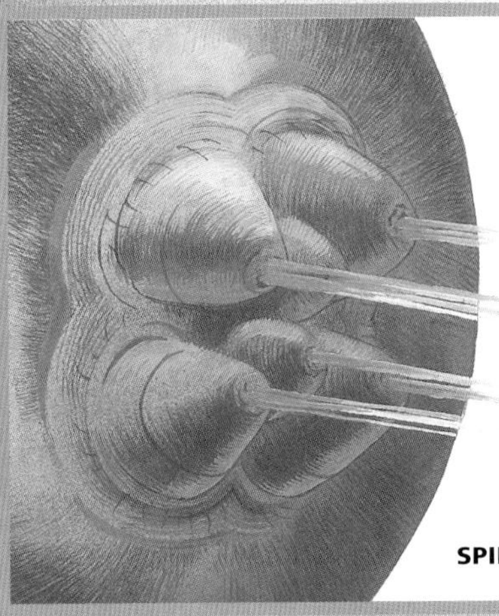

SPINNERETS

When it is pulled, silk becomes incredibly strong. It is stronger than bone and holds together as well as nylon, but is more elastic. A fine silk is produced to wrap up prey.

When the spider senses the prey is caught in the web, it moves in for the kill.

The legs of web spinners have slender delicate tips which sense the vibrating prey.

Webs are unique in the animal kingdom. No other animal has such an enormous catching device!

The circular web spinners are the second biggest group of spiders after the jumping spiders.

LOOK AGAIN!

The redback spider uses hairs under its fourth leg to throw silk at prey.

The Scottish king Robert the Bruce watched as a spider climbed and fell over again and again, until it reached its destination. This inspired him to keep trying until he achieved victory in his battle against the English in 1306.

Web weavers

The 'traffic' of pollen-hunting insects flying through the air was just too much for spiders to ignore. Making sure they could catch some of this rich food supply encouraged spiders to experiment with many different aerial nets of silk.

Australian redback spider

STRONGER SILK

The first web traps were just a sheet extended from the spider's home. All the silk was the same. Somewhere, somehow—scientists don't know how or why—spiders began building circular, or **orb webs**. Spiders used these circular webs in a variety of ways. Some added to it (some spiders weave a white cross into the web), and others used cunning tricks to lure prey to the web; but the fragile web was hard work to build and big insects destroyed it easily. So silk had to become stronger and venom had to kill more quickly.

A special hair under the claws of circular web spiders helps the tiny claws hold onto the web. Scientists still don't know why spiders don't stick to their own webs!

The webs of widow and redback spiders developed three zones: the tube-like home, a messy tangle, and a special catching zone near the ground with sticky lines of silk.

Making a web

Arachne was a Greek girl who spun such beautiful silk that she felt she was better than the gods. She was so proud and disrespectful that the goddess Athena transformed her into a spider, forever spinning silky webs. The scientific name for spider is Arachnid, named for Arachne.

BRIDGING BIG GAPS

The first thick line of orb webs is pulled from the spinnerets by the wind, much like an arrow shot through the air sticks to a distant branch. Then the spider crosses the gap to anchor another thick line. Back to the centre it goes and drops on a safety line to the ground, where it pulls tight on the second loop. Next comes the spokes, the rough spiral, and finally the slow fine spiral with gooey drops of silk. The spirals are evenly spaced at the centre. It all takes about thirty minutes. Twenty metres (65 feet) of silk is used.

A drop of silk carries the web to a far-off tree

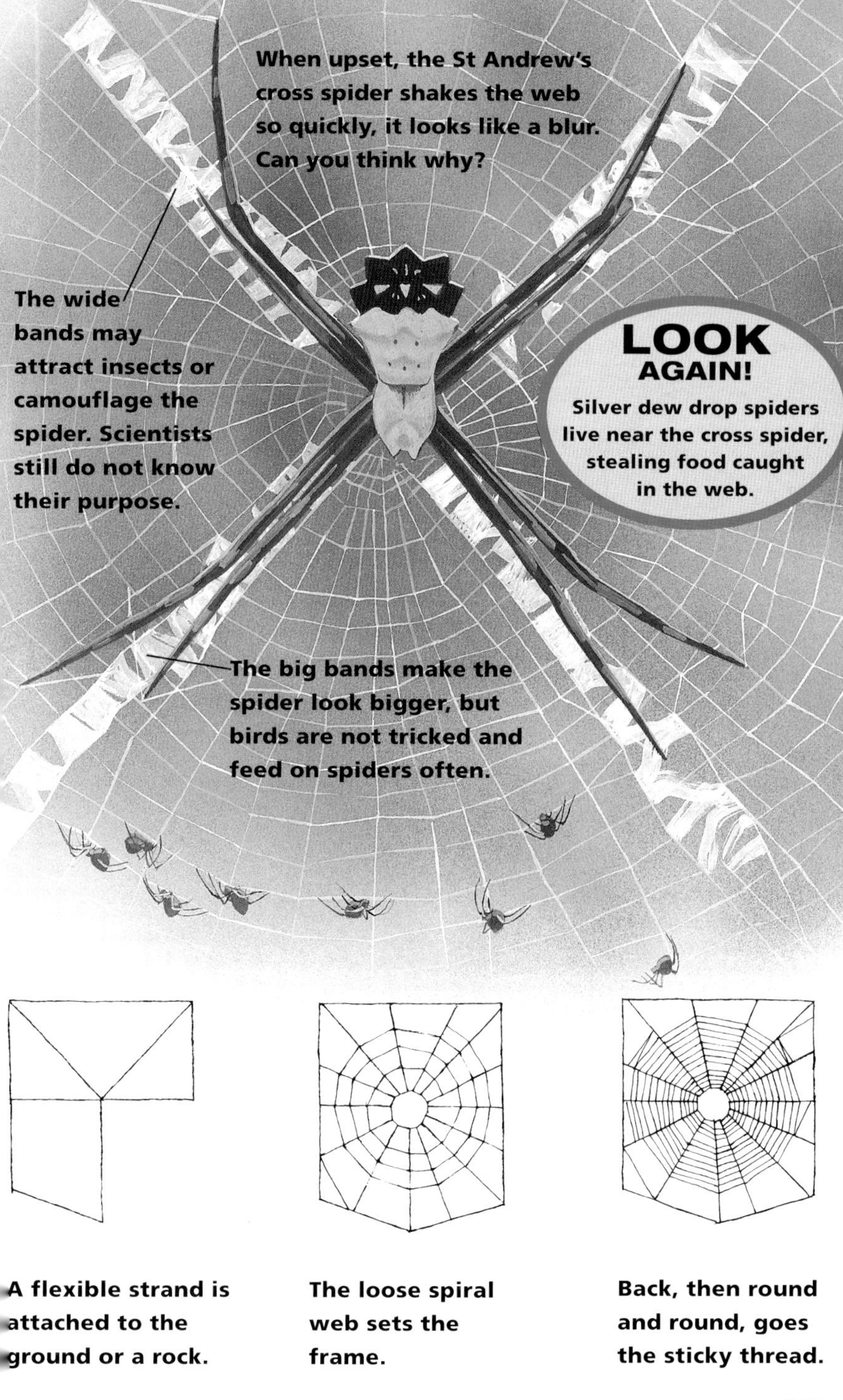

A flexible strand is attached to the ground or a rock.

The loose spiral web sets the frame.

Back, then round and round, goes the sticky thread.

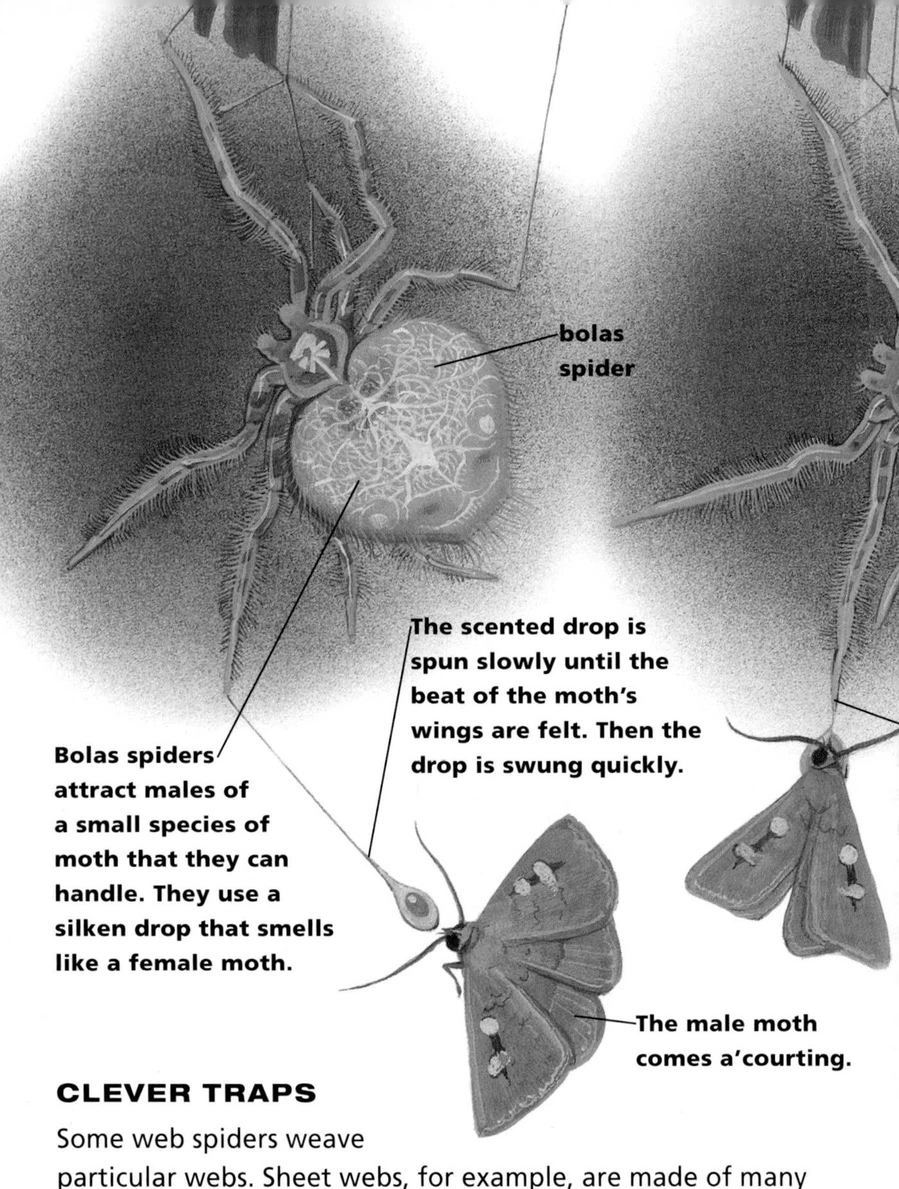

CLEVER TRAPS

Some web spiders weave particular webs. Sheet webs, for example, are made of many threads that cross each other so closely that prey is easily caught. Scorpion-tailed spiders have a piece of fluff on the tail to waggle in the air. Some spiders use camouflage to look like big animals with giant eyes. Many spiders stick mud, dirt or bark to the body and legs and hide on the ground. Some jumping spiders look and move like fluff in the wind and pounce on other unsuspecting spiders.

Catching tricks

In every family (spider and human) someone has to be different! Some spiders have special shapes so they are camouflaged, some make bad smells, some fake death and some use cunning web tricks. Special tricks attract special food.

LOOK AGAIN!

The bolas spider has no web. It hangs from safety lines attached to a branch.

Net-casting spiders hang upside down and hold a silken net between their four front legs. When an insect walks under the net, the spider quickly drops the net over it.

he moth is aught by the ticky drop and he spider pulls he line up to at its catch.

net-casting spider

All those babies!

Mating is dangerous for many male spiders, because they can be mistaken for dinner! To show the female that he is not food, the male must perform a special dance. The mating dance of each species is different. When two males meet, they do a fighting dance.

NURSERIES AND PIED PIPERS

After mating, the male dies. Sometimes he is eaten! Females soon lay eggs on a silk sheet and wrap them in a coloured sac. Giant golden orb-weavers bury the egg sac. Water spiders carry the sac in their fangs and make a nursery for the young. Baby huntsman spiders follow the mother along a web line which she has made to send them off into the windy world. Baby spiders are called spiderlings.

Wolf spiders carry the egg sac on their spinnerets and then the babies cling to special hairs on the mother's back. After only one week, the babies must run for their lives, as they are now food for each other.

MOTHER WOLF SPIDER WITH EGG

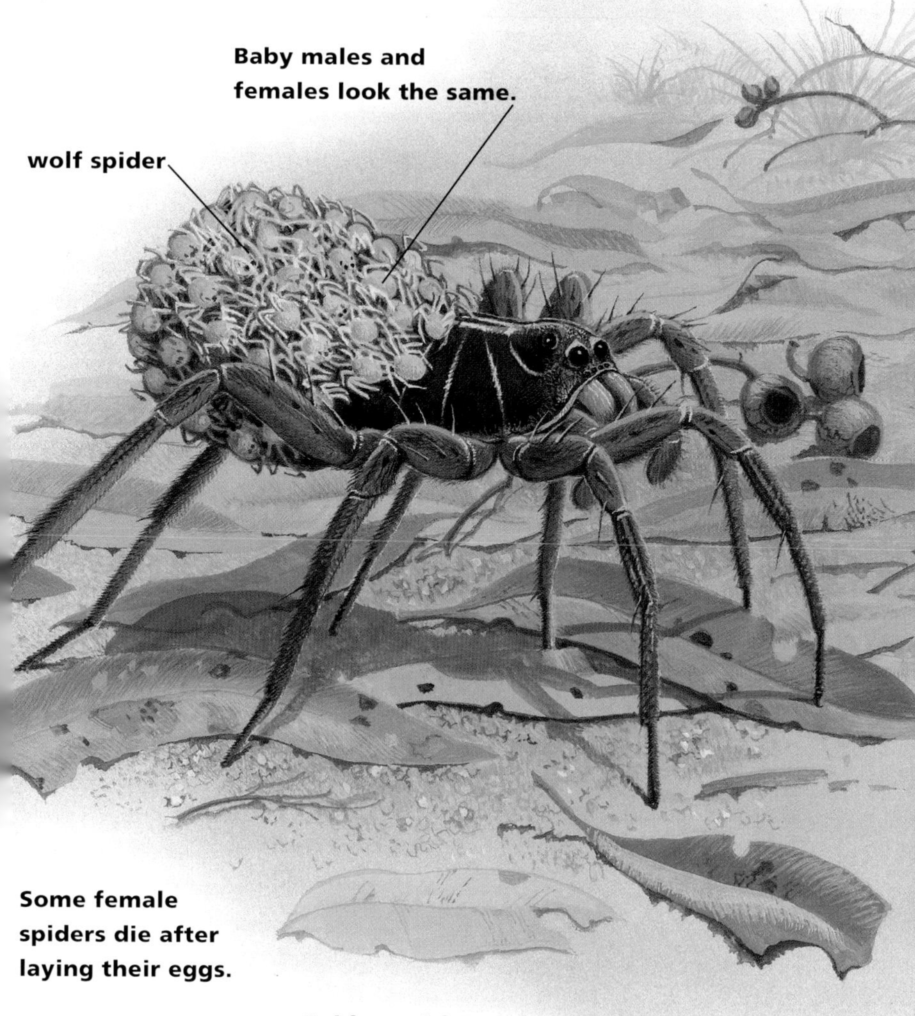

Some female spiders die after laying their eggs.

Spiders with good eyesight have bright bands on the body and legs which they flash during the mating dance.

LOOK AGAIN!

The babies are two or three layers deep and constantly move as the mother walks.

Most spiderlings fend for themselves a short time after emerging from the egg, but some mothers care for their young until they can hunt alone.

Life cycle

Baby spiders in the sac have no colour until they emerge. Then they look like miniature adults. They grow only in the short time after each moult while the skin is soft. Most spiders live for one year, but mygales live for up to 25 years!

A NEW SKIN

Spiders moult or shed their skin several times in their life, even twice before leaving the egg sac. Just before moulting, the skin darkens and the hairs and new skin develop below the old skin. The spider sticks the legs to some silk. Higher blood pressure in the body starts the splits, then the side of the head splits and opens. The new legs, head and body slip out, all soft and pale. The skin dries hard and straight then darkens. Until then, the spider is easily hurt or killed.

1. The spider attaches itself to some silk.

This is a young male—see the bulge at the end of the palp?

Every hair, spine, claw and tooth regrows with each moult!

Spiders drop or lose legs to escape from predators, but lost legs appear again after the next moult. They regrow in the head

LOOK AGAIN!

Most spiders hang upside down when it is time to shed their skins.

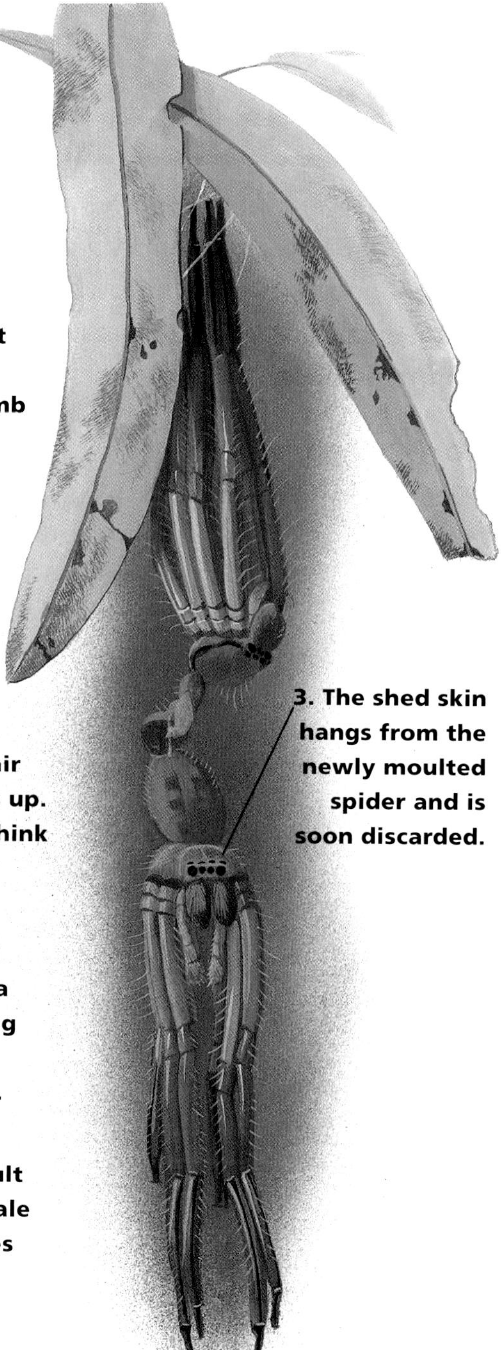

Tarantulas moult on their backs! These giants climb out of their skin and dry slowly.

2. The head starts to split.

Spiders often moult when air pressure goes up. Why do you think this is?

3. The shed skin hangs from the newly moulted spider and is soon discarded.

Many spiders grow and moult several times in a year. They stop moulting as adults when their mating organs develop.

Mygales spiders become adult in about seven years. The male then mates and dies. Females moult and grow for about eighteen more years!

Where do spiders live?

Spiders live and hunt on mountain tops and the world below, under sea and under snow, by lake, by sea, in cracks of soil and slimy mud, in flower, under bark and rock and between all the leaves. From high in the sky to the reef depths, spiders can be found!

ADAPT AND ADJUST

Spiders have evolved and adapted to harsh and strange homes. Littoral spiders live in tubes where ocean waves crash on the rocks. Marine spiders live in air bells deep under coral reefs. Intertidal trapdoors live in lobsters' mud mounds in mangroves. Many spiders live and hunt in the space between snow and the ground. The mudwallower lurks in the sloppiest mud around! Spiders can also adjust quickly when they land in strange new places. The Australian redback (widow) quickly adapted to Japan's icy climate and Belgium's wet conditions. It is also happy in the hottest deserts.

A bubble of air is carried by the spider to the underwater nest. The spider walks through the water but also does 'dog paddle'.

Redbacks can survive one hundred days without food. One was once found happily nesting inside a sealed candy Easter egg. Watch out!

LOOK AGAIN!

The legs of the water spider carry no air. If they did, the spider would only float!

Special hairs on the body
help trap the air bubble.

The garden orb feeds on a juicy moth caught in the night.
Triangular spiders were once orb builders but now hunt free. They have strong, spiny front legs.
Green spiders, like this huntsman, hunt in the day.
The yellow crab spider matches the flower's colour and catches an unwary bee.
The sharp body spines of the jewel spider will stick in a bird's throat.

In the garden

Because the garden environment is often green and damp, there is a lot of food there. Spiders are attracted to the flowers because of the bees and butterflies that come to spread the pollen.

A FEAST IN THE FLOWERS

Flowers are usually planted close together in the garden, so insects are more plentiful than in most forests. Spiders often match their colour to those of the flower or plant. Some spiders' bodies go green from eating bright green grasshoppers—the food shows through the spider's thick skin! In the garden, night spiders curl up under a leaf in the day and build big webs or hunt freely after dark.

Wolf spiders are particular about where they live and they only hunt close to home. Some live on rocks near the water, some live in the grass and others live in the areas between rocks and grass.

LOOK AGAIN!

The pruning scissors were left outside overnight. See the jewel spider's web?

Down the tube!

Trapdoor, funnelweb and tarantula spiders live in burrows. A burrow is cool, moist, dark and quiet—and it's home. A burrow can give a history of the spider's life as it contains bits and pieces from its past. Some burrows have a back door as well as a front door.

BUILDING A BURROW

Spider mothers suspend their egg sacs like a hammock at the bottom of the tube. Newly hatched spiderlings build burrows near the mother's burrow when the ground is soft during light rain. The burrows are enlarged over time. The door is also enlarged and the various building stages can often be seen. The spider binds cast-off skins or moults, old food skins, old egg sacs and even an unlucky dead male into the burrow wall.

LOOK AGAIN!

All spiders line their burrows with silk. This helps keep the soil out.

trapdoor spider

Only a few legs hang out of the burrow.

A smart spider leaves the smelly beetle alone.

Before pouncing, the spider holds the door closed with its fangs!

The purseweb trapdoor spider feels the European wasp walking across the ground. The wasp is then ripped through the burrow wall.

The spider drags the wasp down the burrow to eat it. Later, it will repair the rip in its trap.

FRONT AND BACK DOORS

The doors of a burrow can be separate or hinged. Thick doors keep out rain and unwelcome predators. Some doors are hidden down or off the tube, but it is the main way out. So some spiders have back doors too. They can escape through hidden entrances near the trapdoor. Centipedes seem to know that. They burrow through the soil, then attack the spider through the bottom of the burrow.

House guests

For spiders, houses are just special caves where the wind is slow, the moisture good and the food laid on! Spiders find many places to live, especially in the winter cold and the summer heat.

SNAP, CRUNCH AND SLURP

In the corner of a cupboard, a tiny spider catches ants, silverfish, flies and cockroaches. Watch out little spider! Here comes a wasp. The wasp's trembling legs confuse the spider and it is stung. The spider's legs are cut and its still living body remains fresh food for the wasp's one larva. A swift centipede sweeps through narrow spaces and clamps another house spider hard in its giant jaws. Look up! Above the ceiling is an opening where spiders live and hunt, out of sight of people.

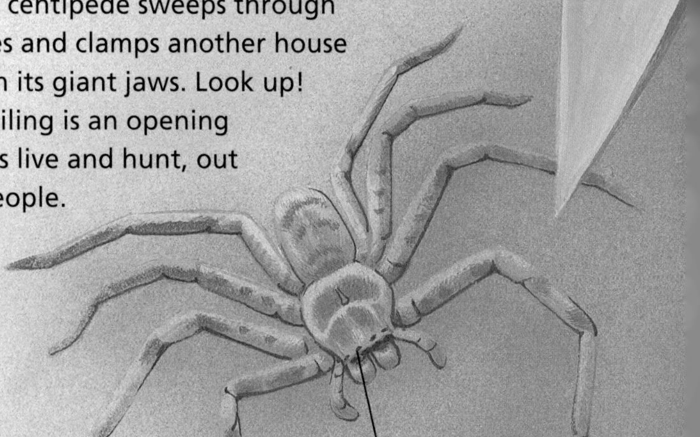

Large huntsman spiders are very sensitive to wind (don't sneeze!), so they hide behind paintings against walls. Fine hairs on their legs vibrate wildly with a little breeze.

Huntsman spiders are nocturnal, or night hunters.

Small moths and other insects are caught in the delicate web of the daddy longlegs spider.
This jumping spider is about to snap the fly's shell, crunch its head, and slurp its body liquids.
LOOK AGAIN!
The jumping spider camouflages itself against the soil in the pot plant.

PLACES WITH SPACES

Forests are places with many spaces—big spaces between trees and tiny spaces in the soil. Spiders specialise in living in specific places called niches. Different spiders explore the bark of dead trees and living trees. Mushrooms and fungi on dead trees attract beetles and flies, and forest spiders hunt these creatures. There are mud-wallowing water spiders. Some make webs and others hunt on the water.

The giant water spider is waiting for her tiny mate.

orb-weaving spider

Water spiders like to eat fish, frogs and insects.

Water spiders lift themselves off the water and sail across.

Forest dwellers

Up to 300 species of spiders live in any one forest. They explore every nook and cranny that we can think of, and many that we can't!

LOOK AGAIN!

The tiny *Curimagua* lives on the mouthparts of big curtain-weavers!

Goliath hunts the forest floor and the trees, taking ground birds and bats on the wing.

Funnelwebs occur only in Australia. About forty species of widow spiders occur around warmer parts of the world.

Funnelwebs don't feed on big animals, and it is just an accident of nature that their venom is dangerous to us!

The body of a female funnelweb is about 35 millimetres (1½ inches) long.

Funnelweb venom doesn't hurt dogs, cats, mice or rabbits. Can you think why not?

The funnelweb venom stops the millipede from squirting its nasty defensive juices.

Dangerous spiders

There are over 35,000 named species of spiders! Almost all have venom, but only about 100 species around the world are highly venomous to humans. Most of those species are Australian funnelwebs, black widow species or fiddlebacks. Most spiders do not occur near us and really very few species are particularly dangerous. Danger is a mixture of opportunity and toxicity!

TAKING CARE!

In Sydney, Australia, many people have made homes right where funnelwebs are very common. Funnelweb venom evolved to kill insects and millipedes. It paralyses them. When funnelwebs bite monkeys or humans, it causes our body to tremble so that we can't breathe and our heart shivers instead of pumping. In Sydney, people must take care at night when the dangerous male goes walking around and into houses.

Widow spiders also like being near us but it is the bite of the female (not the male) widow that is more dangerous. Scientists have developed medicines that can prevent death if a person is bitten.

WIDOW SPIDER

Protecting spiders

Different spiders make different chemicals, have different silk and different venom. They use different tricks to catch different prey. Scientists have studied the chemicals made by spiders and found that some are important to humans.

PEST CONTROL

Spiders eat many kinds of insects. They can help control insect pests in the garden, in the fields and even in the home. If there were no spiders, the world would be overrun with insects. Spiders also teach us about nature, about survival in a harsh world. For instance, sometimes spiders kill animals, like birds, toads and snakes, to stop them breaking their web. They don't eat them because they are too big.

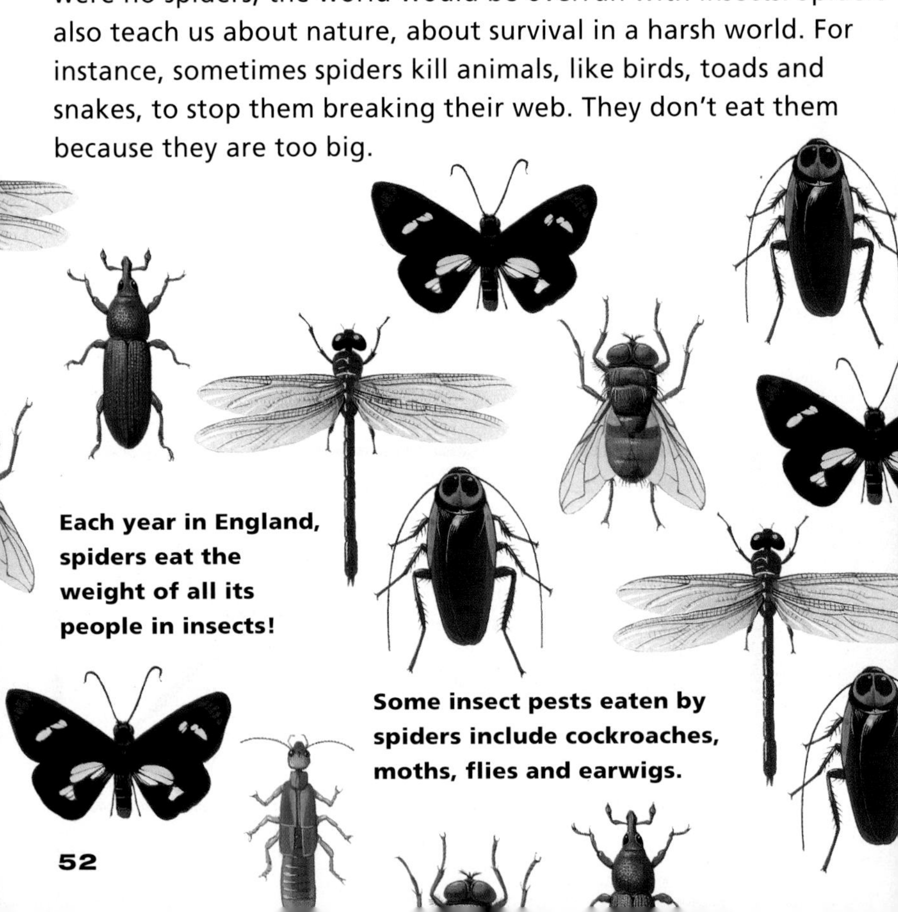

Each year in England, spiders eat the weight of all its people in insects!

Some insect pests eaten by spiders include cockroaches, moths, flies and earwigs.

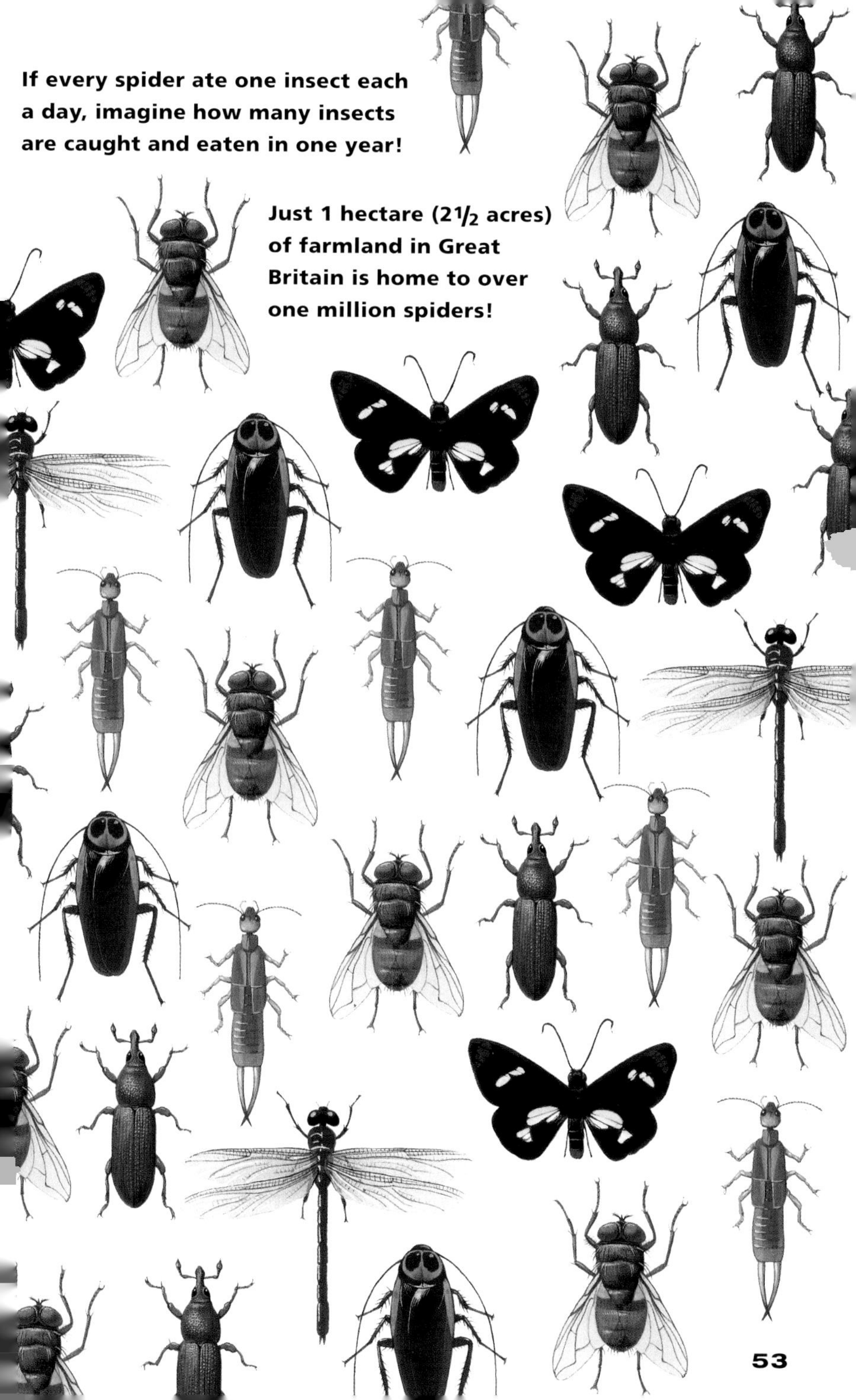

If every spider ate one insect each a day, imagine how many insects are caught and eaten in one year!

Just 1 hectare (2½ acres) of farmland in Great Britain is home to over one million spiders!

ALL SHAPES AND SIZES

Some spiders have long spinnerets. Some have short spinnerets and tiny eyes. Spiders that now, or once, built orb webs belong to one group of families. Huntsmen and crab spiders belong to a group with backward, crab-like legs. Jumping spiders have big eyes and jump. Like huntsmen, they have claw tufts. Wolf spiders have big eyes but no tufts.

Sorting out spiders

Spiders belong to several distinct groups depending on the way the fangs work, the number of lungs they have, the eyes, and how they hunt. Bird-eating spiders, mouse spiders and other mygales have four lungs, long palps, and fangs that bite down.

The best soccer goalie ever?

Imagine a soccer team of spiders! The game would have to be played at night or the goalie would hide! They can't let the web builder make the net, or the ball would stick to it.

SOME GOALIE!

The goalie doesn't need gloves because her feet are covered with dense pads of hair that stop the ball. Does any team have a chance of getting the ball through? Maybe, because she is the slowest player, and she can't move sideways. She can't see the ball, especially standing up like that, so she must keep moving her legs and hope she stops the ball.

Make your own bouncy spider

1. **Take a strip of elastic about 30 centimetres (12 inches) long. Hold one end and mould it around a handful of plasticene or playdough. It's a good idea to tie a knot at the end of the elastic.**
2. **Keep moulding until you make a round shape. You can make it more colourful by painting it, or by putting strips of different coloured plasticene on it.**
3. **Take eight pipe cleaners and stick one end of each into the spider's body. Remember to put four on each side.**
4. **Hang the other end of the elastic in a doorway and frighten your friends!**

The mouse spider is so tough and slow that the other team can easily bounce a ball off her.

The jumping spider and the wolf spider are the only ones that will see the ball coming before it hits them!

GLOSSARY

abdomen (AB-doe-men) The usually soft baggy body. It contains the heart, the lungs, the gut, eggs, and silk-making glands.

arachnophobic Having a fear of spiders.

book lungs Two or four patches that are underneath the body of the spider. They have many thin leaves like a book and help the spider to breathe.

camouflage (KAM-a-flahzh) Colours, patterns or body shape helping an animal blend with its surroundings.

carapace (KARRA-pace) The hard shield over the head.

cephalothorax (KEF-aloe-THOR-ax) The front part of the spider, or head; the legs and **chelicerae** are attached to this.

chelicerae (KEY-liss-err-ee) The two bumps on the front of a spider that move the fangs to bite.

claw tufts Dense pads of hair near the claws that help the spider hold slippery insects and also help it climb up smooth slippery leaves and branches.

cuticle (KEW-tickle) The 'skin' of the spider which can be hard, like on the legs and head, or soft, as in the body parts and joints. It is shed with each moult.

daddy long-legs The name used both for a very harmless spider and a harvestman, which is an arachnid without a waist.

environment The features of the place where an animal or plant lives that influence the way it lives.

evolve To change through generations. Animals and plants usually evolve to better adapt themselves for the environmental conditions in which they live.

fangs The two big sharp spikes at the front of the spider that bite and inject the venom.

funnelweb spiders In North America and Europe, these are delicate spiders that are harmless; they build sheet webs with a funnel-shaped home. In Australia, the name funnelweb applies to very dangerous, large, black trapdoor spiders. It is only the hidden part of its web that is funnel-shaped.

gland An organ that produces a special liquid. Some make only silk, some make only venom, and some make only stomach juices.

larva A young insect, also called a grub or maggot.

lyriform organ A tiny organ shaped like a musical lyre that helps the spider know when its legs are in a bad position.

moult The old, shed skin of a spider.

mygale (MY-gail) A word for trapdoor, funnelweb and tarantula spiders with fangs that work like snake fangs—straight down.

orb web A web that is circular, with a spiralled line of sticky silk.

palp A short way of saying **pedipalp.**

paralysis When an insect (or other animal) cannot move but is still alive.

parasite An animal or plant that lives and feeds on or in another organism without killing it.

patella The spider's knee. This is the shortest joint of the leg.

pedicel (PED-ee-sell) The waist that joins the **cephalothorax** and **abdomen.** Blood and food and sometimes tubes of hair pass through it.

pedipalp (PEE-DEE-palp) The first pair of leg-like feelers at the front of the spider's body. They are missing one segment that the legs have. In males, they are a special shape for mating; in females, they look like short legs.

predator An animal that kills and eats other animals.

prey An animal that is hunted and killed by another animal for food.

spiderling A baby spider.

spinnerets (SPIN-err-ETTS) Up to eight, but usually only six soft bumps on the end of the body that the liquid silk comes through from the glands.

FIND OUT MORE ABOUT SPIDERS

BOOKS

Clyne, Densey, *Spotlight on Spiders,* Allen & Unwin, Sydney, 1995.

Filmer, M. R., *South African Spiders,* Struik Publishers, Cape Town, 1991.

Forster, R. R., and Forster, L., *Spiders of New Zealand and their Worldwinde Kin,* University of Otago Press, Dunedin, 1999.

Hillyard, P., *The Book of the Spider: From Arachnophobia to the Love of Spiders,* Hutchinson, London, 1994.

Hunt, Helen, *The Puffin Book of Australian Spiders,* Penguin Books, Melbourne, 1982.

Levi, Herbert W., *A Guide to Spiders and their Kin,* Golden Press, New York, 1968.

Parsons, A., *Amazing Spiders,* RD Press, Sydney, 1990.

Roberts, M. J., *Spiders of Britain and Northern Europe,* Harper Collins, London, 1995.

WEBSITES

The Arachnology Homepage
http://www.ufsia.ac.be/Arachnology/Arachnology.html

The Queensland Museum Explorer
http://www.qmuseum.qld.gov.au/nature/arachnids/arachnidswelcome/html

INDEX

Page numbers in *italic* type refer to illustrations

INDEX

INDEX

FREE INVESTIGATE POSTER!

Collect 6 of the gold INVESTIGATE stickers

(you will find one on the stickers' page in each book).

Send all 6 stickers on a sheet of paper along with your name and address to:

Investigate Series Poster
Whitecap Books
351 Lynn Avenue
North Vancouver
British Columbia
V7J 2C4

and we'll send you your free INVESTIGATE series poster.

Please allow 21 days for delivery.